Tanja Pajic was born in the second half of the past century, in what was a small village, and is now a part of a city. She acquired good schooling, studying philology and philosophy at Belgrade University, France; Montclair State College, and Rutgers University in the USA for her MA. She returned to her native country and started as a lecturer of Latin and French languages. After working as a publicist, she began writing poetry and short stories; she has published a few of them with success.

Tanja Pajic

DIVERSITY

AUSTIN MACAULEY PUBLISHERS™
LONDON • CAMBRIDGE • NEW YORK • SHARJAH

Ordering Information
Quantity sales: Special discounts are available on quantity purchases by corporations, associations, and others. For details, contact the publisher at the address below.

Publisher's Cataloging-in-Publication data
Pajic, Tanja
Diversity

ISBN 9781643788371 (Paperback)
ISBN 9781643789156 (ePub e-book)

Library of Congress Control Number: 2022913144

www.austinmacauley.com/us

First Published 2022
Austin Macauley Publishers LLC
40 Wall Street, 33rd Floor, Suite 3302
New York, NY 10005
USA

mail-usa@austinmacauley.com
+1 (646) 5125767

Thanks to my colleagues from medical school; my friend
from Association of Writers, Belgrade and Kragujevac,
and to my friend, Sasa, and my parents.

It Is a Morning

It is morning
One old woman hurries
Second old woman hurries
Third old woman hurries
All women hurry
To the market place
In the large street
Car accident;
Six of them injured
How? Talk to the old women
It is market day
They are in a hurry
In the large street
It is market day.

As a Script

As a script on the sky
As a snowman stays
In garden for children
Car on the street
Go fast, go nowhere
Snowman stays with
Its fingers on me
And a car go fast
It is true, one car
Is missing
On the way
To hospital
On the large road.

I Know

It is nice
You love me
It is nice that machine
In front of me
Is writing a letter
Because you love me
As a letter in my hand
I couldn't touch your face
It stays in chip
But I know
You love me.

A Machine

You respond on everything I ask
With your intelligent brain
More than ordinary
Since
You are only a machine
That I am asking
About
Someone.

It Happens

Whatever, it happened
Maybe there is a reason
For saying this
We are in there
We are broader than the universe
And whatever happened
Is for saying this.

Sorrow

Shape is empty
Shape is plain
What is the shape
Emotions in the end that
Follow us
Emptiness in the body
That guides us
What is the shape
A mirror that we belong.

Measure Is "Number One"

Measure one
Measure two, measure x
For how long
In the time
We measure how
Measure is relative.

We Run

Fast, fast, faster
The car is running
Autocar is running
Plain is ruling
Fast, fast
We are as two
Immobile leaves
That wind cannot push
Running.

Soul

The soul is of God
The Gods are
Far from man
And the soul
Far from me
So far that
I cannot reach her
For never, but
My soul is with me,
And God is so far.

Look on You

Sunshine in the mist
Curious weather
Seaside empty
Because it is noon
But you, my love
You stayed on the shore
Caching the last foam
In the ocean
Searching from my eyes.

They are gone in
This curious weather
Gone in the mist
And transfer in the sunshine
Taking a look on you.

Dream

I had one dream tonight
When I saw the mist outside
The moon as blue
As blue as my blue dream
Blue as a red sky
Through the windows
When your voce comes up
Beside the moon that transmits it.

Yellow

Yellow, everything is yellow
In the summer, in the autumn
It is a wood or seaside
Is this a new dress of thy hair
Is something, as a moon as the sun,
Is this a high age or a youth,
What is that on the picture
This is a picture of steel life,
One apple that is yellow, in a quarrel.
Is the blonde hair of her
No, it is only nature that laughs at me.

Love

Far it is
The star of desire
Someplace in the galaxy
They are watching us
And far away you are
Thinking about my life
Thinking but your star
Passed away long time
Begot to me,
Why?
It is a fault of
The galaxy star.

Vagabond

We look at the end
Two little vagabonds
To save our mind
From this world.

You are so little in the sky
I don't exist
We are two travelers
Up to the last man
When we disappear
In vastness of the existence
As a vagabond skips
In the corner of the street.

One Event

As the way of the stars
Goes to our head
You mean that is wind
You keep in your hand
The sky is great
In the evening when you sleep
The universe is with you.

No

May I say?
No!
To say just a word
No!
But a word about you?
Oh, say it
I am a loser
That is not
I am lost in stars on the sky
Maybe the Parqués did not love me
And your destiny?
It is better, but
No, don't say anymore!

Path of Mine

We are walking
Nowhere nowadays
With a smile
We cannot stop
We are walking
Quickly, slowly
But the road is one
Leads us to happiness.

Love

This evening, the Luna
Starts her dance
With her girls in the
Sky
With a shepherd searching for her
Hidden behind a
Moonlight river, the girls
Devouring the shepherd because
He was a beautiful boy
Refusing Luna's love.

Hidden As It Is

Some stars, little shameful
Stay behind a tree
On the leaves that start to be yellow
Searching the stagnant place
To deposit her arrow
Because he was in love with the cloud
That hid her from others.

For Remembrance

Hercules, a strong baby
You mean that birth
Is just from you
As Ahcil, your mother did a sin, but is that love
You little Hercules, when you are grown
You will feel the all disasters of human kind
and God reverence and you will be the first
Leading your soldiers in the sky
Looking down on the Earth.

Sleeping Souls

Traveling souls,
You go some other place to sleep as a
Fanned flower
Until one day, you'll be awaking
Starting again your travel
When we are going
You know
By the way…
When do you go
Eh, if it is over there, I'll be far away
But
I don't go, I am sitting
I am thinking
Is that a meditation
No simply, it is that
It is your body that is hidden from me
As your mind that provokes the mystery
Where are you going from my mind
Everywhere
But I am late
I must go.

Thinking

When we did talk, you did say
What for when we know everything
I did keep quiet
Then you say
You know, you are better than that
I try to say something
No, you are the same.

Yes, we are together
In some space, in some time,
As a to beein wander trouth the wird
Thinking of echo
But never be together.

Only Way

As you mean that is the end
It is the only way
Of becoming
A new way of the thinking
Of ours
Of me and you
As we start to be lovers.

Faraway Voice

I am hearing the voice
I am thinking
It is from far away
And suddenly
A wind opened the window
That was your voice
That comes to me
From some foreign place.

A Store

Luxurious, important,
You stay plenty of light
In the middle of the street
Come the people to buy your fruitful
Assortment of…
Now it the night
You, so outrageous
So lonely
So impoverished of the light
You stay in the dark
Plenty of empty shells…
Tomorrow…
Again a luxury, light, people that hue
I pass every morning early in the town…
Nearby your imposant dwell…

I Know

Suddenly a touch of wind
Got to my hair
I was surprised
The kind nearby did play
And I saw his hand toward me
I saw, I saw, I know it
That was an orphan,
As long as he was sitting
In the corner
In the dust
I saw, I know that I saw
Happiness in his eye,
A hand that touched my hair
A penny that he was keeping
And a shiny voice
"Goodbye Madame."
I know, I know.

No Isn't Machine

Way of our being is a curious machine
That we transplanted into other
As machine
That take from us only one question
Who is machine?
Both are machines
No one is a machine
Machine is a cell that puts
The wire running.

Regardless

Regardless the science which is sprit
It is one other way
Which is sense
Regardless the science which is spirit
We examine
Only a sense with the spirit.

Fantasy

Cosmos in my room
As wind is triggering
My thoughts
That stay far from fantasy
But they are just an open reality
To someone.

Close to mind
Close to senses
We are still on the open road
Of undeniable.

On Man

Misty cloud be one man
He think of himself enviously
But the gods don't open to him.
Did you stay aboard lonely in the dark?
No
I did stay aboard in light
And the glance
Have you passed it?
No I did stare within
Two borders.

Unreadable

But they are so incredibly dark
They are not a ring of lord,
They are slaves on the Planet Earth that
Is going to incredible disaster of
the human sense and
Brains that flew in the airs,
As a ball that I leave the corner of the football,
The minds that were floating there and were
Making one simply incredible…

Eve

One eve, we don't sleep
Street. No empty.
One wood, old in time
Of past
Stays alone
No cover of glittering pomp
No cover of light booths
Just a lonely street
In the suburb
An old tree
Stays alone
It is eve.

Vacarm

Vacarm. One man did bouchaa
Some guns are chutting
It is a pub or a hotel
We don't know yet
Car of first aid will run
What is a purpose
Probably he is still alive
On the door they carry
a corpse of a woman
Beautiful woman.
Vacarm.

Future

Still we think of the future
Or even of the past
In reverse.
Man in future is as one O
On the coordinate
We think of ourselves
But what is the purpose
Just to put more dark
Seeing in dark room.

If We Say

If we say that we know ourselves
Our skin and bones react
With pain that is clashing
Not a brain
But
Senses
It is painful we rethink
And our body grows as to expose
We think and we are suddenly down
We are from skin and bones.

Friends

If we say that we are lonely
Don't trust our words
Because we are friends
Of our thoughts
We are together with
We are thinking
Solely for our friends.

I Can

You never say I can
Because it is unpredictable
Because we cannot say
To anyone that we can
But only to ourself.

Does

Does is not a word
Does is not a meaning
Does is when we say
That we are someone
That we are present
That you are a part
That is a little
Does.

OK

Computer is running
We claim OK
The cursor is getting
The wrong way
A monitor is praying
To see the picture
But since a shadowy face
The memory is low.

May We Know

May we know what is light
No we could not
May we know what is God
No we could not
May we know what we are
It belongs to God
But, may we know?

Passing Into Dream

Cloud goes above my head
It is early in the night
It goes in search
To make dark my dream
I am dreaming
That thus it is nowadays
When we start to exist
In the life of crowned bird
As the eternity sings
For us
The latest song of birth
And life
Thus, we suppose
But we are not
Life is as we
Go by
But is a thinking
Of our dream.

Misery

Stars are coming
Early in the morning
Shadowed by the our
Awakening
Saying on the sky
The story of the cloud
That some passed by
Death is a miracle
But still, it is a misery
Of our being.

We Were

Separately we were
Through our thoughts
Our destiny and
Mind
To think that is will
Will is unknown for
We are all that is
Passing by us.
Separately of sense
But bad is
Only that we
Escape.

Call

May I call you
Apart of my timetable
When my pen is resting
A sweetie
As the moon calls stars
In the midnight
To have an eternal game.

Mechanical Writer

This machine is a writer
A chip that blows inside
To collect in his memory
Every thought
To be written.

Phrase

When we say ONE and ONE, we mean TWO
When we say, a TWO and TWO
It means indeterminable
Combination
That led us to unseen
Space of the universe
Thus just too simple
A number.

Clown

Mentally we are clowns
Probably men of means
The power of the mind
Led us to interminable
Paths of bordered
Being.

Best is more
Than a probability
Best is worsening
Of the senses
Good is better
From our living
From our mind and senses
Because it is simply
A way of talk
About myself.

Being is as a past time
Following us
With the mimic of laughter
As a hidden weapon

It stays in our hearth
But is still forgiven
Thinking about our
In conscience existing.

54

Street Is Crowded

It is not a market place
It is not a shopping center
It is midnight
Whether is nice
Ants or little dwarfs
Go there and where
Trying to reach one street
It is already nine past
Suddenly, empty
No one on the street
NO one
But is still
a working time
we run back to work.

Mathematics

Two parallel lines are cut in the infinity
2+2 je četiri 2=2 is four
X(y) X(x) formulas, formulas
Is that the reason that conscience keeps quiet
In the infinity of our senses.

Your Picture

Program is soundless
I seek for you
Your picture stays in chip
Thus I know you
Hello, it is morning
You are gone
I am closing a computer.

Light Machine

Paradigm and phrase
Repressed in the memory
Face with face with eclipse
Computer moves there and where
Twitter moves there and where
Memory comes with light machine.

Good Morning

You said
I turned
Explicit sound
Ecran switched,
You had a time
To greet me
No one responds
Time disappeared
Into the 'tached baton
Of eternal memory that
Is filled up with one
"Good morning!"

www.ingramcontent.com/pod-product-compliance
Lightning Source LLC
Chambersburg PA
CBHW051722050726

47598CB00003B/1002